This book belongs to

_____

This book is dedicated to my children – Mikey, Kobe, and Jojo.
When you are kind to others, it not only changes you, it changes the world.

Ninja Life Hacks™

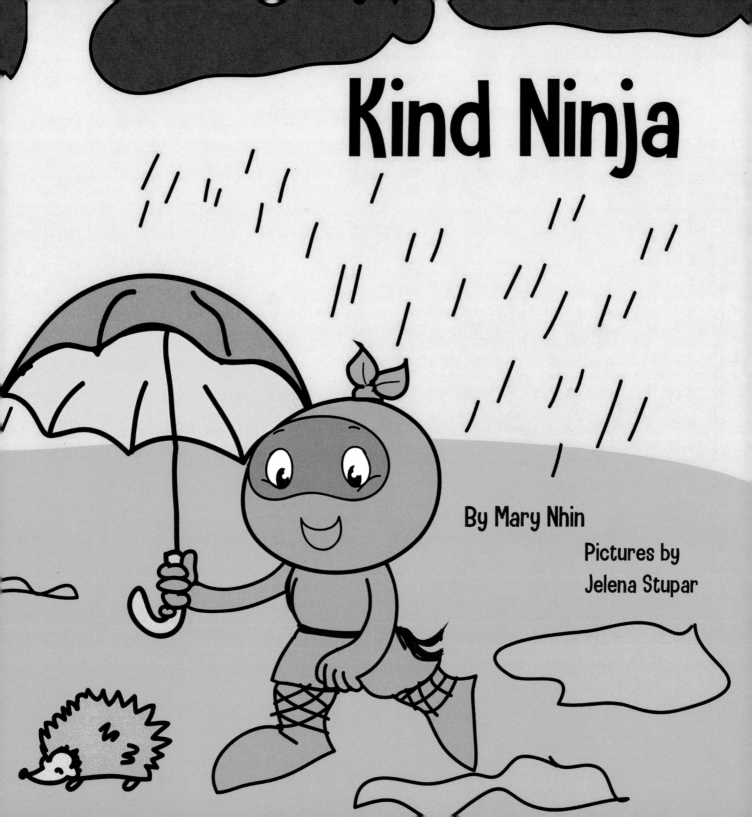

# Kind Ninja

By Mary Nhin

Pictures by
Jelena Stupar

Kind Ninja loved being caring and compassionate.

But it was not always like this. No. Kind Ninja
used to not know any better. It used to be
more about me,

me,

me.

When mom was bringing in the groceries, Kind Ninja couldn't wait to get his snack and play on his phone.

On the way to school, Kind Ninja never thought to share his umbrella.

Heading into church, Kind Ninja would rush in to grab donuts, instead of holding the door open for others or waiting his turn.

But that all changed one day during class.

Anxious Ninja had worked on his science project for weeks. When it was his turn to present to the class, he dropped his entire volcano presentation. Everyone started pointing and laughing, except Kind Ninja.

Kind Ninja could feel Anxious Ninja's pain and embarrassment. He knew how hard it was to get that science project done. And Anxious Ninja's project looked so cool.

He remembered his mother telling him that acts of kindness, both big and small, can make a difference.

Maybe mom was right?

At school, Kind Ninja chose to sit with Shy Ninja, who was sitting alone.

During recess, when Anxious Ninja wasn't picked for a team,
Kind Ninja insisted that Anxious Ninja be on his team.

After school, when all the kids were rushing out the door, Kind Ninja patiently held the door open for Mrs. Payne.

And he shared his umbrella when it rained.

At home, Kind Ninja helped to bring in the groceries.

Brought in the mail to his mother.

And grabbed a bandaid for his sister when she scraped her knee.

POST

Kind Ninja, also, said "Thank you" and "Please" much more often.

Thank you.

Please.

While many other Ninjas were asleep on Saturday morning,
Kind Ninja volunteered his time at the animal shelter.

His duty was to hold the animals and love
on them, but it didn't feel like a job.

Kind Ninja felt lucky to be able to give love and kindness. He liked how being kind made him feel all warm and fuzzy inside.

Simple acts of kindness, both big and small, could become your secret weapon against cruelty in the world.

# Download free printables at NinjaLifeHacks.tv

 @marynhin     @GrowGrit
#NinjaLifeHacks

 Mary Nhin     Grow Grit

 Grow Grit

Made in the USA
Coppell, TX
12 December 2020